The Best Solution to
HUNGER
IN AMERICA

What People Are Saying about this book and about Respecting Our Elders

"While 1 in 7 US Americans experience food insecurity, as much as half of all food produced in this nation goes to waste. We do not have a food shortage problem, rather it is an issue of dysfunctional systems and values around our food and how we care for our children, elders, people experiencing homelessness and all vulnerable people in our communities.

"To many, these grand problems seem unresolvable and hopeless. From 15 years of firsthand food waste activism and food rescue, my perspective is different. Every single US American can have the food they need, and we can end food waste at the same time. This book is both a beacon and a guide for solving these problems, starting in our own communities. For anyone motivated to start a food rescue program to serve their community and Earth, this is the book for you."
— Robin Greenfield, food waste activist, robingreenfield.org

"I had the privilege of supporting the early evolution and witnessed firsthand the ongoing life-transforming benefits this unique food program brought to my life and to the lives of thousands of under-served lower-income people in Marin County, California. If you could use some additional support putting food on the table and are interested in finding a viable way to do so for yourself and for others in your community, this book is a must-read for you. Filled with time-tested strategies, insights and practical tips, this book spells out in an easy-to-read format how this extraordinary charity, Respecting Our Elders, has set up and run a fresh-food rescue program since 2005 and how you could create one in your area, too!"
— Debra Eve Price, former Respecting Our Elders board member, volunteer, and recipient

As a volunteer and fan of Respecting Our Elders for several decades, as well as an ongoing donor, I know the model well and have seen miracles happen. Not only can our recipients feed themselves, but they can share with friends and family, bringing

abundance and plenty to a population that would otherwise be just scraping by or going hungry. Plus, perfectly good, nutritious food does not go into the landfill! The Respecting Our Elders model for ending hunger in America is elegant, simple, and it works!
—**Lindy Woodard MD**

"Ruth, I want to thank you for all your kindness and generosity you showed us all in your distributing food here at our senior mobile home park. It truly is a shame that there is so much waste and yet so many starving worldwide. I do think it's great for those like you who are volunteering your time and energy in making a difference in people's lives."
—**Elsie, a Novato resident**

"The work of Respecting Our Elders is invaluable. For the past 13 years, we have seen how extra food from this all-volunteer organization has helped many lives. In fact, we witnessed how the food became essential for cancer patients during their treatments as food in itself is medicine. Because of the free food received, several of the afflicted were able to become cancer free. Respecting Our Elders has definitely saved lives, and this is a wonderful act and irreplaceable legacy. Thank you Curt and Ruth! You are the best!"
—**Jackie & Randall Lee**

"When I was researching various food related nonprofits, I came across Respecting Our Elders. Ruth Schwartz, their President, offered a ride along with her on some food runs to experience first-hand how they operate. What I discovered was a small, nimble organization who shares good food through caring to know the needs of their donors and recipients. It is an all-volunteer organization with a passionate volunteer staff and leadership driven to serve their community. I immediately knew this was the model I was looking for. Ruth has continually been an inspirational resource for our organizational needs as they arise."
—**June Michaels, Sonoma Food Runners**

"I admire what Respecting Our Elders is doing. They have found a way to solve several problems at once. First feeding hungry people and reducing food waste; creating community by involving the people who receive the food in the program. I started working with Respecting Our Elders in 2009. First as a recipient, then as a volunteer picking up vegetables from a local farm. Most of the participants are elders, but all are welcome. Everyone helps set up, unload and assists with clean-up. We all get to pick out food to take home for ourselves and our neighbors, creating a lovely community."
—**Kathleen O'Neill, Bolinas Community Volunteer**

"Becoming a volunteer has put me on the front lines in the battle against food insecurity. In these times of severe cutbacks to Government grant programs, the Respecting Our Elders model proves beyond a doubt the importance of an all-volunteer organization, where, for example, the volunteers have the opportunity to get food for people they care about. This book is a clear, concise blueprint for how to set up and run such an organization."
—**Larry Savoie, Respecting Our Elders board member and volunteer**

"We have been with Respecting Our Elders for many years and so appreciate the opportunities they have provided for us to help feed needy folks in Mill Valley from our Saturday morning food pantry. Without the expertise of the Respecting Our Elders leadership, we would not have had this opportunity."
—**Kent and Katie Philpott, Miller Avenue Church ministers**

"I've had the pleasure of knowing Respecting our Elders for many years and their dedication continues to inspire me. Their all-volunteer food rescue program is a true example of community compassion and efficiency. The impact they've made in Marin County is remarkable and this book beautifully captures their work. This is an inspiring guide for anyone who wants to make a difference in their own community."
—**Pam Anderson, longtime fan**

"Respecting Our Elders has been a true blessing to our family for the past seven years. Their unconditional kindness, dedication, and generosity have not only helped feed us during difficult times but have also filled our hearts with gratitude. Through their example, my children have learned that giving to others nourishes the soul just as much as it feeds the body."
—**Paul Sterling, a proud father of two**

"This system teaches how to *do community in the most direct and impactful way*—at the dinner table. It was so easy to set up this food program in new areas. I was amazed at how we could quickly establish then manage the pick-ups and distribution schedules. And seeing the communities remember how to take care of each other, remembering the meaning of *neighbor*, was encouraging!"
—**Rua Necaise, Associate Producer Planet Earth Arts, former Respecting Our Elders Board Member and volunteer for over a dozen years**

The Best Solution to
HUNGER IN AMERICA

How to Set Up and Run an All-Volunteer Community-Based Food Rescue Organization

Ruth Schwartz & Curt Kinkead

Wonderlady Books
Novato, California

Copyright © 2025 by Ruth Schwartz and Curt Kinkead

All rights reserved. No part of this publication may be reproduced, distributed, or transmitted in any form or by any means, including photocopying, recording, or other electronic or mechanical methods, without the prior written permission of the publisher, except in the case of brief quotations embodied in critical reviews and certain other noncommercial uses permitted by copyright law. For permission requests, write to the authors at ruth@respectingourelders.org

Respecting Our Elders
respectingourelders.com
ruth@respectingourelders.com

Published by:
Wonderlady Books
Novato, California

Ordering Information:
Quantity sales. Special discounts are available on quantity purchases by corporations, associations, and others. For details, contact the "Special Sales Department" at the email address above.

The Best Solution to Hunger in America/ Ruth Schwartz & Curt Kinkead. — 1st ed.
Names: Schwartz, Ruth, 1945- author. | Kinkead, Curt, author.
Title: The best solution to hunger in America : how to set up and run an all-volunteer community-based food rescue organization / Ruth Schwartz & Curt Kinkead.
Other titles: Hunger in America
Description: First edition. | Novato, California : Wonderlady Books, [2025] | Includes bibliographical references.
Identifiers: LCCN: 2025925011 | ISBN: 9780989038843 (paperback) | 9780989038874 (ebook)
Subjects: LCSH: Food relief--Handbooks, manuals, etc. | Food banks--California--Marin County--Management--Handbooks, manuals, etc. | Respecting Our Elders (Organization) | Hunger--Prevention--Handbooks, manuals, etc. | Nonprofit organizations--Management--Handbooks, manuals, etc. | Voluntarism--Management--Handbooks, manuals, etc. | Food waste--Prevention--Handbooks, manuals, etc. | Social entrepreneurship--Handbooks, manuals, etc. | Sustainability. | Social service--Management--Handbooks, manuals, etc. | Poverty--Prevention--Handbooks, manuals, etc. | Homelessness--Prevention--Handbooks, manuals, etc. | BISAC: SOCIAL SCIENCE / Poverty & Homelessness. | POLITICAL SCIENCE / Public Policy / Social Services & Welfare. | BUSINESS & ECONOMICS / Nonprofit Organizations & Charities / Management & Leadership.
Classification: LCC: HV696.F6 S39 2025 | DDC: 362.5--dc23byla

Dedication

This book is dedicated to the recipients, volunteers, food donors, and financial supporters of Respecting Our Elders, along with Vic Baranco and the rest of our friends at Turn On to America.

Without all of you, the programs and practices we describe in these pages would not exist, and we would not have the experience and knowledge to educate communities across the country about this unique style of food program.

Acknowledgements

This book has been at least ten years in the making, although we have been talking about creating a handbook about how we do our particular kind of food rescue program since our founding in 2005. It has finally come together thanks to several key people who have drafted various chapters and provided feedback and other content. Big thanks to Fay Freed, Gabrielle Javier, and Larry Tackett, as well as the entire Respecting Our Elders board of directors, and the beta readers who took the time to give us such excellent feedback.

Table of Contents

Foreword 1

The Respecting Our Elders Story 5

Winning the War Against Hunger 9

Introducing a Whole New Kind of Food Program 13

What Exactly Is a Food Rescue Program? 19

Why There Is a Need for Our Kind of Food Rescue Program 21

Getting Food 23

Distributing Food 29

Working with Volunteers 35

Getting Donated Vehicles for Your Organization or for Select Volunteers 41

Farmer's Markets 43

Discover Your Appropriate Organizational Framework ... 47

Fundraising 51

Marketing & Communications 55

Conclusion 61

Sources & Further Resources 63

Foreword

America is the richest country in the world, yet food insecurity continues to rise. In 2023, over 47 million Americans—one in seven households—struggled with consistent access to adequate food. That included nearly 14 million children, over a third of single-mother families, and a disproportionate share of Black and Latinx communities. Rural areas carry a heavy burden, and teachers across the nation report too many students arriving at school hungry.

Older adults face a growing share of this struggle. In 2022, nearly 7 million seniors were food insecure, and 10.2% of Americans age 65 and older lived below the official poverty line. Under the Supplemental Poverty Measure—which better accounts for medical and housing costs—that number rises to 14.1%. Without action, Feeding America estimates that over 9 million seniors could face food insecurity by 2050.

Here in Marin County, the problem is especially pronounced. Our county has the fastest-growing senior population in California, and according to a 2014 Marin Grand Jury report, 69 percent of seniors are at high or moderate risk of poor nutritional health. We are the very people who built this community—working, raising families, contributing to civic life. Yet as we age, health challenges and reduced income often strip away the security we once had. The need for local, dignified solutions is greater than ever—a challenge that conscious and caring people cannot ignore.

I came to this work with deep roots in hunger relief. In 1988, I led the People-to-People Initiative (PPI) for The Hunger Project in the United States. That effort emerged during a period when President Reagan dismantled much of the social safety net put in place under President Johnson. Food programs, mental health services, and other supports were defunded or closed. Families lost cash assistance and Medicaid, pushing them deeper into poverty. Reagan's 1981 budget cuts to food stamps and welfare alone removed billions of dollars from households that needed it most.

The Hunger Project, which had focused internationally on ending starvation, recognized that America was now in crisis. The PPI was created to help communities "take care of our own." Within two years, over 300 communities were networking to support their neighbors. One of the central questions we asked was: "Who is our own?" At first, people thought only of those who looked like them, but week after week, we challenged that notion. We came to see that the elderly widow living on reduced Social Security, the mother sleeping in a car with her children, the man struggling with opioid dependence after surgery, the family buried in medical debt—these were all "our own." Hunger was in every community, affecting people who lived, worked, and raised their families right alongside us. That realization was empowering. Once we expanded our definition of community, we could truly make a difference.

That lesson remains vital today. Our country is divided politically, religiously, and economically. Yet hunger knows no ideology, religion, or moral stance. It affects millions on the economic margins, and the dismantling of federal supports, combined with stagnant wages and inflation, leaves more people vulnerable.

This is why I have supported and volunteered with Respecting Our Elders since its inception in 2005. Ruth Schwartz and Curt Kinkead had already worked with food recovery programs before moving to Novato in 2004. Seeing the opportunity with a new Trader Joe's opening, they asked to pick up food that was still edible but unsellable—ripe produce, food at or close to their sell-by dates, day-old bakery goods, and other surplus items. What began as one pick-up a week quickly grew into two, then many more, because the stores trusted Ruth and Curt to show up, treat people with respect, and ensure the food went directly to those in need.

From the beginning, they recruited volunteers from the recipient base, many of them lower-income seniors. This simple but profound choice meant that people were not just passive recipients of charity; they became active participants in building community. Respect was at the core of the program. Volunteers were treated as equals, and in turn, they found meaning, exercise, social connection, and dignity through service. It was not only about saving food, but about dignity. People moved, as Ruth and Curt often say, "from needy to greedy to generous."

Today, Respecting Our Elders is an all-volunteer nonprofit with no paid staff and an annual budget of just $25,000. Yet it distributes $4–5 million in food annually, serving roughly 1,000 households each month. This is food that would otherwise end up in landfills, costing stores tens of thousands in disposal fees and adding to environmental waste. Instead, it nourishes people, builds relationships, and saves resources. Everyone wins. The program has earned an outstanding reputation with its partner stores. Because Ruth, Curt, and the volunteers never fail to show up—even on holidays—the stores know they can rely on Respecting Our Elders. When other organizations falter, they call on this group. That consistency has built a 20-year track record of trust and impact.

Ruth and Curt deserve utmost recognition and praise for spearheading this model and effort for two solid decades. The results go far beyond food. For seniors, it reduces expenses, improves nutrition, and relieves loneliness. For volunteers, it provides purpose, connection, and physical activity. For the broader community, it builds resilience, environmental responsibility, and the simple joy of neighbors helping neighbors.

I've seen many hunger programs come and go over the decades, and I can say without hesitation that this model is one of the most effective I have ever encountered. Ruth and Curt had the vision and perseverance to create something truly extraordinary. They designed a program that is lean, replicable, and deeply human.

This Foreword isn't just statistics—or history. It's a rallying cry and an invitation. Food insecurity in America is increasing.

The Best Solution to Hunger in America

Behind each number is a neighbor, a parent, someone whose life would be drastically changed if they could receive some extra food on a regular basis. That food is available in the back of every grocery store in America. It just needs someone comsitted to picking it up and distributing it. That's exactly what programs like Respecting Our Elders have proven possible — transforming waste into nourishment and ensuring no senior — or anyone else in need — in our community is left hungry. This book, The Best Solution to Hunger in America, is a detailed manual that will guide you on how to create an all-volunteer, people-oriented food rescue program in your community.

—Larry Tackett
Member of the Board of Respecting Our Elders
Former U.S. Director, The Hunger Project's People-to-People Initiative

Introduction

The Respecting Our Elders Story

Long before we founded Respecting Our Elders, we had been involved with other food programs that focused on picking up surplus food that was still perfectly edible and getting it to people who could use it. This was (and still is) food that is dated and needs to be pulled from the shelves, produce that is a little too ripe, or packaged goods that have been slightly damaged but are still quite usable.

A Little History

When we moved to Novato in January 2004, we had already been bringing food to the residents of the Villas at Hamilton at the center of Hamilton Field. A friend of ours who lived there had also participated in one of the same food programs and knew that several of his neighbors weren't getting enough to eat. With rents at this "affordable housing" complex eating up most of some residents' Social Security income—plus the cost of medications thanks to Medicare's "donut hole" system—there simply wasn't enough left for good-quality food.

One resident, an elderly woman with no family, was living on three potatoes a day. This was unacceptable to us and our friend. In 2003, Curt would roll up in his pickup truck filled with fresh produce and other good food, and the residents would gather to "shop" from the truck. This continued even after we moved to the Villas in January 2004.

When it was announced that Trader Joe's was opening in Novato, we decided to set up our own nonprofit, with the goal of picking up food from the new store when it opened in 2005. We secured one day a week, then a second (Sunday), which the Food Bank declined to cover. From there, the program expanded to include

The Best Solution to Hunger in America

all three Trader Joe's stores in the area, several Safeways, and then one, two, and eventually three Whole Foods stores.

From a Truckload to a Movement

Things have shifted since those early days. Today, more than 75 volunteers from our all-volunteer nonprofit pick up from three Whole Foods stores, two Trader Joe's stores, three other grocery stores, and the Civic Center Farmers Market.

Respecting Our Elders primarily deals with fresh food. Whatever we pick up is delivered immediately to people who can use it. In essence, we are a "garbage prevention operation," rescuing food that would otherwise be trashed due to being close to its sell-by date, slightly damaged, or overripe but still edible.

No Barriers to Access

There are no qualifications to receive food from Respecting Our Elders. People self-qualify. If they feel they could use some extra food, even temporarily, they are welcome to attend an open food day or receive food at their senior complex. This contrasts sharply with programs that require proof of income and distribute pre-selected boxes of food regardless of personal preferences. This self-qualification also extends to the charity's volunteers. (More about this in Chapter Seven (Working with Volunteers.)

Our model allows recipients to "shop" from a wide variety of fresh produce, prepared foods, gourmet breads, and pastries—essentially, a selection that mirrors what you'd find in the donor stores.

What Makes This Program Different

From day one, Respecting Our Elders was designed to be more than a food distribution program. We created a true community effort. We chose to operate as an all-volunteer organization with no paid staff, ensuring that all funds went directly to supporting the work.

But even more innovative was our choice to recruit volunteers from within the recipient base. Lower-income seniors—people who understand what it's like to need a little extra help — are the ones distributing food to their peers. This shared experience creates a sense of dignity, compassion, and empowerment that is rare in traditional food programs.

Over time, participants shift from scarcity to sufficiency, even to a sense of abundance. Generosity becomes contagious.

Community from the Inside Out

No large-scale aid program can truly meet individual needs, even though individuals make up 100% of their intended recipients. Aid programs aim to be "fair" through uniformity, which often results in inefficiency and missed opportunities.

In contrast, our model allows for targeted, compassionate support. A grandmother with a son out of work can immediately begin helping his family — with the full support of her community. This isn't limited to relatives. Any volunteer can choose to help anyone they come across who could use some extra food to make ends meet.

That flexibility and humanity make this program unique. The community distributes the food. And when problems arise, they're addressed on a case-by-case basis — not with blanket rules or rigid bureaucracy.

Transforming Lives

Today, our program feeds between 500 and 1,000 people each week, mostly underserved seniors in Marin. Many would not qualify for food stamps. Thanks to Respecting Our Elders, they are better able to cover rent, medications, and occasional outings with friends.

Above all, the program fosters community. Entire senior complexes now function more like extended families, organizing themselves around the food deliveries and finding new purpose in the process.

The Best Solution to Hunger in America

Built on Sustainability and Trust

All of this has been achieved with minimal funding. We are supported primarily by individual donors, with occasional microgrants from stores like Whole Foods, local banks, and small foundations. Respecting Our Elders receives no government funding. As Curt is fond of saying, "This program doesn't cost the taxpayers a cent."

And yet, crises have arisen. When the van used for pickups and deliveries blew its engine, the community rallied to raise $6,000 in less than a month. Since then, we've established a $25,000 annual Sustainability Fund to ensure the program can keep going even when unexpected costs arise.

A Model for the Nation

We are always looking for more food donors. We're ready to expand because the need still exists—especially among seniors. Donating food reduces landfill waste, saves stores money, and boosts morale among store employees who know they're making a difference.

As stated on our website, our mission is to:

- Eradicate hunger and poverty in Marin while building community
- Help food purveyors lighten their environmental footprint
- Provide a replicable model for communities across the United States

Everything we pick up is delivered right away. We don't store anything, so no warehouse is needed. And many of our volunteers have been with us since our founding in 2005. This model can be duplicated anywhere there's a grocery store and a willing community. We hope it becomes the new standard for food programs nationwide.

Chapter One

Winning the War Against Hunger

Food scarcity isn't the problem — it's distribution. There is no true shortage of food in this country — hunger exists because of distribution issues. In Marin County, the 2012 Marin County Food System Assessment Project concluded (see Sources & Resources: Marin County Food System Assessment Project):

"There is more than enough healthy food to end hunger in Marin County.... It is a distribution and re-purposing challenge — not a supply issue."

The Scope of Food Waste in the United States

We toss out nearly 30–40% of the food supply, and food is the single largest material in U.S. landfills. Most of this waste is still perfectly edible.

- The EPA estimates that 30–40% of the food supply is never eaten (see Sources & Resources: EPA, USDA, RTS) — food that could be redirected to help neighbors in need.

- Another source reports Americans discard almost 40 million tons of food yearly — about 325 pounds per person.

- Additional estimates from the USDA highlight similar figures, reinforcing how widespread and costly this problem is.

Government Support Is Waning

Federal food assistance programs are under increasing strain due to recent funding cuts to food banks and similar services. This makes community-based efforts like ours even more vital in ensuring people don't fall through the cracks.

An Untapped Solution: Rescue and Redistribute

What if there were an easy, low-cost way to take all of that food that stores are tossing into dumpsters and then into the landfill, and get it directly to people who can use it? We are not just talking about the people who qualify for government food programs, or the people who are willing to line up at agencies feeding the hungry, like St. Vincent de Paul, or even the local food banks, or the agencies supported by those food banks.

There is a whole segment of our population that, if they have access to abundant, free food, could most likely make ends meet on their fixed incomes (usually just Social Security). These are the seniors in your area who want to stay in their homes or at least stay in the area where they have lived for many years, or they have come to your area because their kids and grandkids are living there.

Although Respecting Our Elders does wind up feeding very low-income folks, including some homeless, the main segment of our recipient base are these seniors who are seriously challenged to make their money stretch to just cover housing and medications. We have seen many instances of seniors going hungry because their dollars just did not go far enough to put enough decent food on the table.

"Ruth, I want to thank you for all your kindness and generosity ... It truly is a shame that there is so much waste and yet so many starving worldwide."
— Elsie, a resident in Novato

Feeding Others in Need

In addition to seniors, people are living in your area who for various reasons (out of work, outrageous medical expenses, or on disability), if they had access to this food for as long as they needed it, could make ends meet, and they could start moving out of just surviving to being less stressed and even start having some fun in their lives. Perhaps these people are the grown children, with their own kids, of seniors in your community who, all of a sudden, have landed on their parents' doorstep because they lost their home to foreclosure or big rent increases.

Then there are the homeless. Some communities across the country are still faced with homeless encampments or places where the homeless gather. What if there were a way to get food to those people who may not be in that situation due to any fault of their own?

You May Not Be Alone in Your Food Rescue Efforts

Let us hasten to point out that, if you decide to set up our kind of food program, you may not be the only organization providing free food to people with food security issues in your community. There is probably at least a food bank operating in your area, and possibly a food rescue organization or two. In our county, we can eliminate hunger here precisely because of what we are doing in addition to everything else that is being done, and we are reaching segments of the population that either don't qualify or don't have access to the other programs in Marin.

Respecting Our Elders has been a true blessing to our family for the past seven years. Their unconditional kindness, dedication, and generosity have not only helped feed us during difficult times but have also filled our hearts with gratitude. Through their example, my children have learned that giving to others nourishes the soul just as much as it feeds the body.
— Paul Sterling, a proud father of two

Triple Benefits, All in One Program

Here's what happens when a community adopts this model:

The Best Solution to Hunger in America

1. People in need get nourishing food.
2. Perfectly good food is kept out of landfills.
3. Local stores save on dumpster fees and earn goodwill.

Plus, we've seen that when food rescue programs take root, crime rates can dip, street solicitation often declines, and community spirit rises." Interested? Keep reading.

AT A GLANCE

- Hunger in America is caused by distribution problems, not food shortages.
- 30–40 % of food is wasted — most of it edible.
- Local programs can redirect surplus food to neighbors in need.
- When food rescue programs take root, communities grow safer and stronger.
- Everyone benefits: People eat, waste drops, stores save money.

Chapter Two

Introducing a Whole New Kind of Food Program

First of all, let us spell out exactly what makes this food program unique and why it works as well as it does.

An All-Volunteer Charity

We set up Respecting Our Elders as an all-volunteer charity for two reasons: We wanted to have this nonprofit be a "by the people, for the people" kind of organization, and because we did not want the hassle of having employees — even if they were us.

By all of us being in this together (founders, board members, volunteers, and even recipients), we make this about sharing food as a community, not about having a strict hierarchy. Yes, of course, we, as founders and board members, have leadership roles, but that does not take away from the community flavor. Also, it means that we don't have to raise money to pay one of us or someone else as the Executive Director. As a result, our budget is about $25,000 a year on average, which makes our fundraising a lot easier than other nonprofits. Your budget might be even less, depending on whether or not you decide to reimburse volunteers for mileage or gas. (See Chapter Ten on fundraising later in this book.)

Because we are an all-volunteer organization and do not pay salaries, we don't pay into Social Security, Worker's Compensation, and more. And because our gross income is less than $50,000, we can file a Form 990N instead of the far more complicated Form 990. ($50,000 is the current maximum for Form 990N.) Our state, California, has a comparable system for nonprofits, as yours most likely does, too. This keeps things simple in terms of our bookkeeping and paperwork/online filing, etc.

The Best Solution to Hunger in America

We strongly recommend that you take this same all-volunteer approach. Of course, that decision is yours to make.

Volunteers Are Selected from the Recipient Base

We make every effort to do this because then we know that our volunteers don't only care about those they serve, but they have a deep-felt compassion for them, since they are or have been in the same situation regarding needing some extra food to make ends meet. As a result, Respecting Our Elders is, and has been since its founding, an ongoing source of joy for all involved.

Basically, we are the first charity of, by, and for poor people, as Curt Kinkead is fond of saying.

Volunteers Get to Shop from Whatever Food They Are Picking Up and Delivering

This is one of the biggest differences between our food program and every other one out there—and we have looked all over the United States! Our volunteer positions are offered primarily to people who are themselves recipients. We look for those who really want and can help or they need a lot more food than they could normally get from us for two very important reasons: it is the best way we could think of to guarantee that all of us have true compassion for those we serve, and letting our volunteers help themselves to as much as they want of whatever they want makes theft impossible and guarantees that they will go through everything and at least look at everything to be sure that it all looks at least partly edible while doing their personal shopping.

What we have noticed, however, is that our volunteers only take what they need for themselves, their families, and/or people they know who could use some extra food but cannot get direct access to our programs. And if they need more than a reasonable amount from any one load of food, we offer them additional volunteer slots on other food runs.

For example, back when we started at the Villas at Hamilton, one of the residents was actively helping unload our pickup truck, and we noticed that every so often, he would take a box of food over to his car instead of into the basement, where we were distributing the food. We asked him what he was doing, and he explained that his mother was in a nursing home, and he wanted to do something nice for the staff there so that they might take better care of her. We made other arrangements for him to get more food.

Occasionally, we attract volunteers who are as passionate about this program as we are, but they really don't need food for themselves. However, we always encourage them to look around their lives for people they know who would welcome some extra food so that it would be easier for those folks to stretch a meager budget.

What this means is that we have (and you can too!) the world's happiest and most dedicated volunteers. Some of our volunteers have been with us since our founding in 2005, and most of them have been with us for years. This privilege of being able to get food for themselves and others around them is the key. And the volunteers who want to help just to do good (and not get food for themselves or others) don't stay with us very long.

People volunteer for this kind of program not only because they get to make other people's lives better (one of the standard reasons anyone volunteers for anything), but also for the value it brings to their lives—and that includes free food! That may sound selfish, but what we observe is that our volunteers are among the most generous people we know, and we make it easy for them to be so generous by giving them access to abundant (mostly healthy) free food to pass on to people in need. Our volunteers get the satisfaction of bringing to others like themselves the program that has so drastically bettered their own lives.

No Need for Recipients to Qualify

We have all had our share of intake procedures and limitations, so our charity has none. If someone feels that they could use some extra food and can make it to one of our giveaways, or lives in a senior complex that receives food from us or just asks to be put on our Saturday bag list, we assume that person knows his or her own needs better than anybody else possibly could, which means we don't need to know anything more about them.

People basically self-qualify. This is in contrast to programs where a senior has to be below a fairly low-income level in order to qualify for a pre-selected box of food, without taking into account their personal tastes.

We feel it is an invasion of privacy to ask people to reveal their income, living situation, expenses, and more just to get some free food. Interestingly enough, since we have come on the scene in our county, many of the places distributing food that comes from the local food bank, including the food bank's own system of community and senior pantries, have stopped asking people to fill out any sort of paperwork or even give their name. It is just more respectful.

Food Goes Directly From Pickup to Recipients

With rare exceptions, every load of donated food that is picked up by Respecting Our Elders goes directly to a lower-income senior complex or an Open Food Day. Currently, there is one exception: At our Saturday Bag Program, the food is gathered at one location and quickly divided into bags. Then the bags are loaded into volunteer vehicles for delivery to recipients. In the past, we have also taken a load of food to an organization whose volunteers buy all of the food to feed over eighty people. We have made it easier for them to pull together those meals that are prepared and delivered to the recipients who have signed up for that program. We have also delivered vanloads of food to places that have a pantry program of their own, adding what we bring to what they get from other sources.

Also, on occasion, if we have too much of something (like bread), or we get a request to pick up after our usual morning schedule, we will take that food to a nonprofit that is feeding people, like a shelter or soup kitchen operation.

The point here is that we do not take the food back to a warehouse to be weighed, counted, and stored, as food banks do, even for distribution the next day. Most of the food we receive cannot tolerate that kind of timeframe. Even if a food bank does include rescued food in their deliveries to their recipient locations, it is already at least 24 hours older than when they picked it up, and at that point, it could already be spoiled, too ripe, or certainly past the "expiration" date on the package. Therefore, it should really be thrown out rather than distributed. So, what is the point of a food bank picking up that kind of food?

Basically, what we are is a food rescue operation. We pick up produce that is too ripe to put out for sale, prepared food that is coming up to or at their expiration date, and grocery items that are being discontinued or whose packaging has been damaged in some way. There are other food rescue groups. However, every other food rescue operation we have heard of — and there are a growing number getting established across the country — takes the food they receive to nonprofits feeding the poor. Now, this is a great thing! However, as we have already discussed, the people we predominantly serve are not the ones who will go stand in line to get a free bag of food or a meal. Either they can't get to these locations, or they don't qualify, or it is too humbling or embarrassing an experience. That doesn't mean, however, that they don't really need some food to make ends meet.

One of the side benefits of targeting these populations is that it keeps them from having to access the services designed for the very low income, and it keeps them in their homes. It is amazing what some free food can accomplish!

"Having a daughter with epilepsy and her two kids (who have developmental problems), along with my son (who was just laid off), all living with us, it seems that money doesn't stretch very far. We are so grateful for the food we get from Respecting Our Elders."
– Susan, San Rafael

The Best Solution to Hunger in America

The above are the key features of our kind of food program. We do want to mention that we made a decision right at the beginning to focus on regular weekly pickups that go to the same destination each week. We currently work with seven grocery stores and a farmer's market operation every week. There is a lot of other food out there that more "traditional" food rescue operations go after, like restaurants, catering companies, hospital cafeterias, and special events. Those types of food donations are not as consistent as grocery stores, and receiving food from them has a different set of challenges, requiring a different sort of system, one that connects volunteers with the source of the food and a recipient organization. By having a set schedule of pickups and deliveries, we can run an operation that distributes over four million dollars (retail value) of great food (average of 250,000 pounds annually), seven days a week, with over 75 regular volunteers, and it runs like clockwork with minimal administrative attention.

AT A GLANCE

- Operate as an all-volunteer organization—no payroll, no bureaucracy.

- Recruit volunteers from your recipient base; compassion drives success.

- Volunteers may take food for themselves and others—this builds dignity and trust.

- Keep systems simple: regular routes, minimal rules, community spirit.

- Respect, reliability, and flexibility are your keys to longevity.

Chapter Three

What Exactly Is a Food Rescue Program?

Also known as a "fresh rescue" food program, what we are doing could be seen as civilizing dumpster diving. However, we eliminate the dumpster and bring the perfectly edible but no longer premium food from the store directly to groups of consumers and individuals for immediate distribution. This is, in effect, a garbage prevention program.

Because the food we give out is technically garbage, in that it no longer has any RETAIL value without further investment in it, it can't possibly affect anybody's standing with any other program and needn't even be reported. This food is totally tax-free to everybody we give it to, for that reason.

How It Works

A food rescue program elegantly circumvents the waste system by intercepting food that is still edible but no longer sellable due to minor imperfections or approaching sell-by dates. This food (in the case of the Respecting Our Elders operation) is sourced from retailers and promptly redirected to those in need through our deliveries to lower-income senior complexes, our bag program, and our Open Food Days. This approach not only salvages good food from being discarded but also supports community well-being and reduces environmental impact.

Here in California, we now have a law in place that covers this type of food program. It is SB1383 (see Sources & Resources: California SB1383). Under this law, the role of food rescue organizations becomes even more crucial. SB1383 targets a significant reduction in organic waste in landfills as part of broader efforts to combat climate change, mandating that edible food no longer destined for sale must be recovered rather than wasted. By 2025, the law required that 20% of currently disposed edible food be recovered for human consumption.

A Legal and Environmental Imperative

For food rescue programs, this law provides a legal framework that supports their activities, emphasizing the need for increased food recovery and redistribution efforts. It also involves a more systematic approach to tracking the types of food rescued and the quantities, contrary to previous practices where detailed tracking was not necessary due to the non-commercial value of the food. Each of the stores we pick up from has its own reporting system, and Respecting Our Elders reports an annual poundage total to Zero Waste Marin, which in turn reports to the State of California.

While the rescued food is still technically "garbage" because it does not possess retail value, it assumes a critical role in the state's strategy to reduce greenhouse gas emissions from landfills. The law implicitly acknowledges the intrinsic value of this food by encouraging its redistribution, thereby affirming that its worth transcends mere market economics. This shift not only helps fulfill environmental goals but also feeds more people without affecting their eligibility for other assistance programs.

AT A GLANCE

- Food rescue is "garbage prevention" — saving edible food before it's trashed.
- This food has no retail value, so it's tax-free to recipients.
- California's SB 1383 and similar laws nationwide now encourage recovery.
- Reporting helps track the environmental and social impact.
- Every pound rescued feeds people *and* keeps waste out of landfills.

Chapter Four

Why There Is a Need for Our Kind of Food Rescue Program

The Problem With Food Banks

The main source of emergency food has historically been food banks. However, for many years, there has been a need to provide food beyond emergency situations. There are people who just need some extra food to make ends meet, to put food on the table while still covering their rent and other expenses. Food banks have also historically been organizations that required people to sign up and provide personal information.

But that is just the beginning of the problem with food banks. They store collected food in warehouses for at least a day before distribution. Fresh rescued food needs to get to people that day. Storing that kind of food for even one day can make it inedible. Salads spoil, and bread gets hard. Yes, canned and packaged goods can be warehoused. But not fresh food. It needs to get to people right away.

Problem with Other Food Rescue Programs that May Be in Your Area

Not everyone lives in groups or can get to a place where they can get a free meal. Other food rescue organizations only deliver to other nonprofits or agencies serving the very poor, or they are sponsored by a church specifically for the church's pantry that individuals can access.

That excludes people who don't have transportation or are homebound. Other food programs may not reach these hidden population segments.

The Best Solution to Hunger in America

Our local food bank, once they saw how effective our direct-to-the-people approach was, set up food pantries at the various senior complexes. However, those pantries just distribute bulk produce (non-organic), bread, and an occasional small selection of other kinds of food. We know because there are a number of these senior complexes that have asked us to come by and take what's left off their hands and find homes for it.

Our Deliveries are Directly to the People

With our system, we can reach a wide selection of people in need. Yes, Respecting Our Elders focuses mainly on lower-income seniors. However, through our Open Food Days and our Saturday Bag Program, and even through our Farmers' Market program, we reach families and individuals. Our commitment is to serve everyone we can.

AT A GLANCE

- Food banks help but can't handle highly perishable food fast enough.
- Rescued food must go straight to people — not to warehouses.
- Many programs overlook seniors and homebound residents.
- Direct-to-recipient delivery fills those gaps and restores dignity.
- Quick, respectful distribution keeps food fresh and relationships strong.

Chapter Five

Getting Food

Respecting Our Elders wouldn't exist without a consistent supply of surplus food from local grocery stores and markets. Enrolling stores as food donors is both simpler and more impactful than many people think. In this chapter, we'll walk you through the key strategies we've used to build and maintain strong relationships with store partners, along with practical tips and insights from over two decades of hands-on experience.

Finding Donor Stores

Start by identifying potential food donor locations:

- New Stores Opening in Your Area: Reach out before they open — they may be more open to partnerships while still building community goodwill.

- Stores Without Donation Programs: Some stores are still throwing away edible food. These are prime opportunities.

- Stores Unhappy with Their Current Recipient Organization: Be professional and non-critical but let them know you can often offer more consistent service.

- Stores with Gaps in Coverage: Offer to cover holidays or odd pickup days that their regular partners can't accommodate.

Even if a store already donates to another group, they might need backup or additional pickups. This is often how we first get in the door.

Making Contact: Approaching Store Managers

There are two main ways to approach store staff:

1. Get an introduction from someone with a connection to the store—an employee, a community member, or even a volunteer who shops there regularly.

2. The Direct Approach: Dress respectfully, bring printed materials, and be ready to explain who you are, what you do, and how it helps *them*.

Bring a folder that includes:

- A one-page description of your program
- Your nonprofit 501(c)(3) letter (or a letter from your sponsor)
- EPA food waste triangle—black-and-white is fine (link to this graphic is in the Sources & Resources section at the end of this book)
- Testimonials or press clippings

Be prepared to talk about scheduling, logistics, and what kinds of items you can take (ideally: anything they think is edible, regardless of sell-by dates or any merchandise that is in good shape). Basically, we tell the stores we will take anything they want to give us. That gives us a tremendous advantage over our competition.

What to Say: Benefits for the Store

- Reduced Dumping Fees: Stores save money by donating instead of trashing food.
- Employee Morale: Employees often appreciate knowing that food goes to people in need.
- Community Reputation: Donating food builds goodwill.
- No Liability: The federal Bill Emerson Good Samaritan Food Donation Act protects them (see Sources & Resources: Bill Emerson Act).

Be Easy to Work With

- Be efficient: Load quickly and clear out.
- Be reliable: Show up when you say you will.
- Be flexible: Work around store needs.
- Be nonjudgmental: Take what they give. If your program can't use it, find another home for it.

We've made a point of accepting more than just food. We also take flowers, over-the-counter medications, cosmetics, household goods, and other donations that bring joy and dignity to our recipients.

What to Expect From Stores

Some stores may ask you to sign paperwork, such as an IRS form or a donation tracking agreement. That's fine — just make sure you understand what you're agreeing to. Each store may have its own system.

Store Pickup Logistics

We recommend two or three volunteers per store pickup. Any more can overwhelm staff. At least one volunteer should have a vehicle large enough for the full load.

Also,

- Wear your organization's name tags
- Follow any store-specific rules
- Keep interactions professional and positive

Why This Model Works

Unlike food banks, we don't warehouse or sort food for later. We pick up and deliver the same day, which ensures freshness. Stores know their donations go straight to real people, often within hours.

The Best Solution to Hunger in America

We also offer something unique: we *welcome* food past its sell-by date, as long as it's still edible. This gives stores more flexibility and means less waste.

We assure stores that we never resell what we collect and that our volunteers treat the process with care. We become their trusted partners.

Farmer's Markets and Non-Grocery Pickups

While grocery stores are our main food source, we also work with:

- Local farmers' markets
- Coffee and tea companies
- Occasionally, one-time donations from events or restaurants

Farmer's market pickups are more physically demanding but offer a wider variety of produce. These are covered in detail in Chapter Nine, Farmer's Markets.

How Much Food Should You Take On?

Start small and scale up. It's better to say no to a donation than to take food you can't distribute. Be realistic about your volunteer capacity, storage options (if any), and transportation.

If you establish a reputation for reliability, stores will often increase their donations—sometimes more than you expect. Always be prepared to expand your team or route when that happens, especially on or after holidays.

A Note on Gratitude

Make sure to thank store managers and employees regularly. Send an occasional handwritten note or small treat from your volunteers. Let them know their efforts matter. Relationships are the heart of this work.

In Summary

Enrolling local stores to donate food to you is easier than you can probably imagine. First of all, assume that you can get any store to give you their donations because you can serve them better than your competition can—in all kinds of ways. If they are currently throwing away their edible food, instead of donating it, find out why. If they are afraid of legal liability, there is a federal statute called The Bill Emerson Act that holds them harmless for any act that isn't deliberately harmful or grossly negligent. If they throw edible food away, it costs them money to add it to a landfill, and most supermarkets can cut their disposal bills in half by donating what's edible.

The food banks are warehouses, and because most of what stores donate is highly perishable, the one thing that food can't stand is warehousing. The food that food banks pick up on Fridays, Saturdays, and Sundays may go straight into cold storage and isn't even seen until Monday morning. That food, if given to fresh rescue organizations like Respecting Our Elders, will be in consumers' hands within a few hours of the time we pick up, not days.

Food banks and most other food rescue programs won't take anything beyond their sell-by date, and grocers know that most packaged perishable foods will still be okay to eat for about a week after the sell-by date. Those other food rescue programs go through all of their donations at the store and leave behind what they don't want for the stores to throw away. We tell the stores we'll take anything they think is still good to eat, and we don't worry about sell-by or use-by dates because they don't really matter. They are just arbitrary dates the producers make up.

The food banks and other food rescue programs only take food items, but we will gladly take flowers and plants, over-the-counter drugs, toys, kitchen utensils, cosmetics, paper goods, and any other merchandise in good condition. Our recipients appreciate those items as much as the food.

The Best Solution to Hunger in America

Another point is that the food we give out goes to the stores' neighbors, who frequently get things they fall in love with, and if we are basically handling their food expenses, they are making ends meet with a surplus. They can afford to buy those things they love so much, which means they aren't having to buy low-margin survival foods; they are buying the high-margin delicacies they have fallen in love with, thanks to you.

Even if your store prospect is already giving its food to another organization, it probably gives its employees holidays off, which means they need someone else to pick up on those days, which is a good way to get your foot in the door. And don't overlook farmers' markets. Those farmers don't usually want to take unsold produce home with them, so they will often give it away.

AT A GLANCE

- Approach potential donor stores with confidence and professionalism.

- Explain the mutual benefits: lower dumpster fees, goodwill, legal protection.

- Be reliable — stores value consistency more than anything.

- Always say yes first; you can redirect excess later.

- Express gratitude often; handwritten thanks go a long way.

Chapter Six

Distributing Food

There are probably any number of ways one could go about distributing donated food. We always felt that one of the beneficial outcomes of distributing food was that it could be an exercise in building community.

Another way worth at least mentioning as a distribution model is to give the food away anonymously. One very successful food rescue organization in the East Bay of Northern California drives trucks to poor neighborhoods, stops the trucks to hand out boxes of food out the back.

Timing
It has been our goal to go from food pickups at stores to delivery into people's hands within four hours and have it all be as pleasurable and fun as possible. For the delivery of perishable items, you can utilize insulated bags, or large coolers with cold packs, depending on available resources.

Finding Groups of People in Need
The real job of food distribution is to identify locations where there are people in need. If you are operating under the auspices of a religious organization, the food distribution may happen right at their facility, in some kind of easily accessible community room.

In our case, as Respecting our Elders, we opted to focus on seniors, as well as setting up a weekly bag program, and some Open Food Days. Many of our recipients live in affordable senior housing communities and can walk to the community room where the food gets distributed. We currently deliver to eight lower-income senior housing facilities.

Part of the magic of any of our programs is that there are no qualifications for taking food. If someone needs food, we will do our best to get them some food.

Some recipients have a little too much money to qualify for access to government programs that require them to have income below a certain level. But what we know is that whatever money they can save on food can help with medication expenses or even allow for some social activities like going out for coffee or a movie.

Bag Program

Our bag program was designed for volunteers to easily bag groceries at a central location and then quickly deliver them to recipients' homes. We have had a church give us space to set up tables and make up about 40 bags of groceries from the food we receive that morning. For this kind of program, you will need to handle your garbage, recycle cardboard boxes, and have a place to take any surplus that is left over after the bags are complete.

Volunteers (some of the same, some different than baggers) deliver the bags to shut-ins who have been identified through social worker referrals, folks in need after hospital stays, and/or friends of volunteers. A bag is left at a recipient's front door, and the volunteer rings the doorbell or knocks on the door. It is the recipient's responsibility to take it from there. The recipients know that their bags will be delivered within a certain timeframe, and they are responsible for being home during that time, bringing the food inside, and promptly putting any perishables away.

We never know what we will get to put into the bags. Our recipients know that, and if there are some foods they don't want, we ask that they share them with neighbors. This is yet another aspect of how we share food as a community.

Open Food Days

These are basically free food pop-ups that can happen anywhere. They can be done in churches, in a field next to a fire station, or at a marina, for example. We do not ask anyone to qualify or even provide any personal information. They just need to show up and follow the guidelines for that particular location.

Often, we partner and collaborate with other groups and organizations to make these happen most easily. The functions of tables, garbage, and cardboard recycling need to be handled. Many hands make light work.

A Fast, Innovative Food Day Distribution System

At most of the senior complexes we serve, and at both of our current Open Food Days, the spirit of community thrives. Although we do not manage the actual distribution of the food at the senior complexes, we do share with them our method of getting a food distribution done within ten minutes from when the food first arrives.

Here's how that works: When we arrive, everyone who is there to get food helps unload the van to the best of their ability. Even the most frail among our recipients can take a small bag or box and get it to a table. We strongly encourage everyone to participate. After all, we are a community sharing food, we are all in this together, and the more people that help, the faster everything gets done. It also gives everyone a sense of ownership regarding the distribution of this food.

Once everything is unloaded, we do our best to make sure our recipients are getting the food they want. The way we do this is we ask everyone not to take anything before we say, "Start." What we ask them to do instead is to find the thing they want the most from what they can see on the tables and put their hand on it. If there is more than one hand, we ask them to negotiate. Then, we ask them to take that one thing. If we have a smaller amount of food on a particular day, then we may go through this choosing process a second time. Then we let people just move around the tables and choose what they want for themselves.

The truth is, the more food we have at each distribution event, the better this goes. Everybody relaxes because they know they are going to go home with a lot of food, all of it of their choosing. And the whole operation takes less than 10 minutes, sometimes

The Best Solution to Hunger in America

including packing up the empty cartons and putting away the tables.

Ruth, I just wanted to let you know that we appreciate all the things you do. My mother so appreciated having something to look forward to every time, and the feeling of her being useful and independent is priceless.

— Resident of Traditions housing development, Hamilton Field, Novato

---

In contrast, at those pantries set up by our local food bank, people have been known to wait in line for over two hours, and then they can only go through the line once and only get one of each category of food. This is sad, and it is pretty standard among food banks in that the goal is to distribute food as evenly as possible, with the idea that this is the only fair way. Since we never know what we will receive each day, there is no way we can divide things up so that everything is distributed equally. It's just not going to happen. And isn't it better that people go home with what they want and not with what is allocated to them?

In terms of the food that is left over from the food bank pantries, fortunately, Respecting Our Elders has arrangements with several senior complexes to stop by after the pantries to pick up this leftover food, which really should have found its way into the hands of people who can use it. Otherwise, it would find its way into the landfill or maybe a composting operation.

In conclusion, a wonderful thing that happens when we share donated food as a community is that it brings people together. It also engenders a sense of purpose, inviting everyone to participate to the best of their ability. This both pushes back against isolation in addition to alleviating financial pressure for folks.

AT A GLANCE

- Aim to deliver all perishable food within four hours of pickup.
- Identify clusters of need — especially senior complexes and homebound clients.
- Encourage recipients to help unload and organize; it builds community.
- Keep it fast, fair, and friendly — 10 minutes or less for a full distribution.
- Share abundance; nothing should end up in the trash.

Chapter Seven

Working with Volunteers

We set Respecting Our Elders up as an all-volunteer non-profit organization with no employees because we wanted to make sure that all of our fundraising efforts resulted in direct support of our programs and not in paying anyone's salary.

In addition, one of the keys to this model of program is that most of our volunteers are pulled from our recipient base, which is primarily lower-income seniors living in Marin County. The recipients are the people who need food themselves. In that way, the volunteers know what it's like to need some extra food and thereby have the utmost compassion for all of the people they serve. Their need for assistance means they find themselves in the same boat as other food recipients..

The overall philosophy of this organization is that volunteers participate as a community, taking care of each other.

What was found time and again is that people moved from living in scarcity and survival to a greater sense of sufficiency and abundance — even to an experience of prosperity — where you are so filled up that you have enough to pass on and take care of others. In fact, we encourage all of our volunteers and other recipients to look around to see who they can help, rather than just focus on taking food for themselves. The focus is always on spreading generosity wherever one can.

Recruiting Volunteers

A really good place to start recruiting volunteers is by looking at the people who are identified as needing food. Also, those who know others who need extra food. Make sure that potential volunteers understand that they absolutely can get food for themselves and for people in need whom they care about (relatives, neighbors, co-workers, etc.).

It is also important to know which volunteers drive cars, vans, or trucks and which do not, since vehicles are needed to be used for food distribution.

And even before recruiting, it is important to know what your needs are for picking up food.

We would recommend sending at least two and not more than three volunteers for each store food pickup. (Sometimes the donor stores can get nervous if more than three people come at a time.) Amongst those two to three volunteers, one of them needs to be driving a vehicle that is big enough to hold a typically sized food donation load.

We would also recommend that you look for people who can be trusted to make and keep their commitments. Or at least to communicate clearly and in a timely manner when something comes up.

Our volunteers are given Respecting Our Elders name tags so that store personnel know they are legitimate and can feel immediately comfortable dealing with them. The store representatives might have specific instructions about how they want the pickup process to go. This might include timing details or where to park the vehicles, etc.

And volunteers need to fill out and sign a Volunteer Agreement. There are two different versions: one for volunteers using their personal vehicles to transport food, and one for the rest of the volunteers.

Managing Volunteers

Over the years, we tried multiple ways to organize volunteers in teams. As we already said, for our store program, there are usually teams of two or three. But sometimes, there is only one person. In that case, they do all the vehicle loading and driving to the recipient facility.

For our Saturday Bag Program, we have a combination of people who are picking up and then bringing the food to a central location (in our case, a local church) and other volunteers who help pack the bags. Many of the volunteers then turn around and deliver bags to the recipients.

With our Farmers' Market program, we have created a system of weekly team leaders and team members. Most of those volunteers do one week a month. For further details, see Chapter Nine, Farmer's Markets.

Acknowledgement Is Key

In addition to all of the free food they get, it is important that they get acknowledged regularly for their efforts.

For example:

- "You are making such a difference in the lives of our recipients!"
- "Thanks for all you're doing!"
- "Thank you for what you did."

Listen to volunteers' experiences, needs, and successes. If someone is unhappy, you need to find out why and resolve the issue. If they are having a great time, then ask them for a testimonial!

The Compliment Sandwich

This practice is based on the idea that we learn faster through acknowledgment than through criticism.

- Part 1 is finding something the volunteer did that was good and acknowledging it.
- Part 2 is requesting nicely that, regarding whatever content, they might be able to do it this way next time.
- Part 3 is acknowledging them when you see them taking action in the direction of the thing you requested.

Firing Volunteers

This is very rare. In the twenty years of doing this work, we have had only two instances where we had to ask someone not to come back. One was where a volunteer kept insisting on entertaining us with his trumpet playing, and the other was with a volunteer who thought she could go by anytime to one of the Whole Foods stores because she knew someone who worked there, and because she was one of our volunteers. In both cases, we used the above Compliment Sandwich process, but after several attempts and their behavior not changing, we had to let them go.

I cannot tell you how much this helped me with my food budget. At the time I found Respecting Our Elders, we had not had a social security increase in two years, our rent continues to increase every year, and gasoline and other expenses also continue to go up. I am not a wealthy "Marinite" and every little bit helps. This little bit from this amazing organization went a long, long way for me.

– Chris S., San Rafael

Volunteer Agreement

In general, managing our volunteers has been an easy process. The initial step is to have them fill out and sign our Volunteer Agreement, especially for people using their own vehicles in service to the charity. One version is for volunteers who do NOT use their vehicles in service to the charity, the second is for those who do use their personal vehicles for the charity, and the third is for Farmer's Market volunteers.

You will find a link to a folder that has PDF and MS Word files of the three agreements in the Sources & Resources section at the end of this book.

AT A GLANCE

- Recruit volunteers from within your recipient base whenever possible.

- Make expectations clear, honor commitments, and celebrate reliability.

- Regular acknowledgment keeps morale high.

- Use the Compliment Sandwich for feedback: praise – suggest – praise.

- Remember: people move from scarcity to sufficiency — and into generosity.

Chapter Eight

Getting Donated Vehicles for Your Organization or for Select Volunteers

Donating a vehicle to your charity can provide the donor with a valuable tax deduction. In most cases, when a charity sells a donated car, the donor may deduct only the sale price — often just $350–$500.

However, we take advantage of a different option. Under IRS Publication 4303, donors may deduct (see Sources & Resources: IRS Publication 4303) the full fair market value (private party Blue Book) if the charity:

- Puts the vehicle to significant use in its program (for example, using it to pick up and deliver food).

- Makes a material improvement (such as major repairs, not just cleaning or painting).

- Donates or sells the vehicle to a needy individual at a substantially below-market price if this directly furthers the organization's charitable purpose.

For food rescue programs, there are two common ways to meet these requirements:

1. Direct Use by the Charity — The vehicle becomes part of your fleet and is used by the organization itself to pick up food donations from stores, farmers' markets, or other sources and deliver them directly to recipients.

2. Placement with a Volunteer — A vehicle can be given to a dedicated volunteer who actively participates in collecting and distributing food for the program. This

ensures the vehicle remains in service to the charity's mission

When seeking vehicle donations, be clear about what will be most useful for your operations. Many programs find that minivans or small cargo vans in good condition, ideally with under 75,000 miles, are ideal for transporting food safely and efficiently.

Because these vehicles are put into immediate charitable service—either by the program directly or by a volunteer—donors may qualify for a full fair market value deduction instead of the limited resale amount. This creates a win-win: the donor receives a greater tax benefit, and your program gains the reliable transportation it needs to keep food moving from stores to the people who need it most.

AT A GLANCE

- Vehicle donations can qualify donors for full fair-market-value deductions.

- Use donated vehicles directly for pickups or assign them to active volunteers.

- Minivans or small cargo vans work best—affordable and maneuverable.

- Maintain and document charitable use to meet IRS requirements.

- A dependable vehicle keeps food (and goodwill) moving smoothly.

- Everyone benefits: People eat, waste drops, stores save money.

Chapter Nine

Farmer's Markets

Respecting Our Elders, as we have said, transforms lives by solving the problem of food insecurity. Additional benefits are reduced food waste and healthier community members. With our weekly Sunday Farmer's Market operation, abundance is shared simply: vendors donate, volunteers sort, and recipient groups take home nourishment for their communities.

We are including this chapter on our Farmers' Market weekly event even though it represents only a minor percentage of our overall food rescue operation, maybe just 10%. You may or may not choose to add a Farmer's Market segment to your program. It is a more complex operation than our work with retail stores. Another thing to consider is that it requires more heavy lifting than the regular store pickups as well. However, if you are choosing to do a Farmer's Market stint, below is a general blueprint of how we've run this particular operation. How you set up your own Farmers' Market operation is, of course, up to you. If you want to see the detailed "manual" of how we run our weekly Farmers' Market operation, just ask.

The Operation Is Straightforward

Volunteers arrive near closing time, collect donations directly from vendors, and bring them to a central sorting spot. There, food is divided among the recipient groups and volunteers. The key is efficiency and respect—working quickly so as not to interfere with vendors' peak hours and handling all donations with care. Supplies are minimal: boxes, a tarp to keep things organized, and signs to designate recipient groups. A few carts or hand trucks make collection easier.

The team structure is simple as well. A coordinator ensures each week has enough volunteers and basic supplies, while weekly leaders and volunteers carry out the collection and sorting. Another nonprofit may sometimes join in, and having clear roles and communication ensures everything runs smoothly. Importantly, the recipient groups themselves send a representative to pick up their prepared boxes, but do not participate in the sorting. We've found this prevents misunderstandings or concerns about whether any group is being short-changed, while also keeping the process quick and fair.

This book is so very timely. The discrepancy between haves and have-nots continues to grow. Today's need easily mirrors Depression Era economics. This book offers a detailed template for all communities to put into use while, at the same time, rescuing food and product that would otherwise end up in a landfill!

— Marty Wickenheiser, Respecting Our Elders board member and volunteer

---

The number of volunteers needed depends on the size of the market, but four to seven people can usually cover a medium-sized operation. Many come from the same communities that receive food, which strengthens relationships and builds trust. Word of mouth is the most effective way to bring in new volunteers, and recipients themselves often step up to help in other parts of the program.

As you have read, this chapter is an outline, not a perfect formula. It is built on our experience over the years. As the outline is followed, there may be opportunities to expand or simplify — the journey is yours. The beauty of this effort is that it fosters community at all levels: from laying the groundwork and building teams, to nurturing relationships with vendors and with those who receive the food. This model can be adapted in any community, no matter the size of the market, and always carries the same reward—turning surplus into nourishment and strangers into neighbors.

AT A GLANCE

- Farmers' markets offer fresh produce and direct relationships.
- Keep the process efficient: collect, sort, split, distribute.
- Assign team leaders and coordinate with other nonprofits if needed.
- Be visible and respectful—name tags and clear signage matter.
- Treat donations as gifts; handle all food with care and gratitude.

Chapter Ten

Discover Your Appropriate Organizational Framework

In order to have a food rescue program, you do need the legal structure of a legitimate non-profit to operate within. The reason is that stores will not even talk to you without one.

So then, what are the three ways to operate as a non-profit?

Local Church, or Synagogue, or Mosque

This is the easiest way to obtain a legal nonprofit status. The religious institutions can issue you the necessary paperwork to fulfill the stores' requirements.

They hold the fiduciary responsibility. If you need to raise money, you would do so through their charitable organization. But you may not need to raise money if the volunteers are using their vehicles to pick up and deliver food.

Find a Fiscal Sponsor

Some organizations operate as fiscal sponsors that you can sign up with to have your food rescue program under their auspices. The same privileges, such as raising funds, apply, just as they would in a church situation. Most commonly, sponsors take a percentage of the project's revenue, ranging from 5% to 15%, depending on the sponsor and the services provided. This is commonly referred to as an administrative allocation.

In both cases, those organizations might also have physical space where either an office or food distribution can happen.

Setting Up Your Own Non-Profit

The other way you can house your program's fiduciary responsibilities is to set up your own non-profit 501(c)3 corporation. It is surely the most expensive of the choices.

One needs to work within the IRS and your state's governing laws. It takes both time and money to set it up, but then you are independent of others' conditions and terms. We set up a non-profit called Respecting Our Elders and have operated with that structure now for over 20 years.

How to Set Up Your Own Non-Profit

If you choose to set up your non-profit, there are excellent resources available to help you through the process. Your first step is to check out Nolo Press.

They have one book that applies to all states, as well as other books on non-profit issues that you might find useful. Links to these books are provided in the Sources & Resources section. They are great because they offer sample Articles of Incorporation and sample Bylaws.

For current IRS requirements, see the Sources & Resources section for applicable links.

What You Will Need:

- Articles of Incorporation filed with your state; a link to ours is included in the Sources & Resources section
- Bylaws of the corporation are also required; a link to ours is included in the Sources & Resources section as well.
- A Board of Directors needs to be established, with a minimum of at least three distinct individuals. A President, a Treasurer, and a Secretary.
- Certain types of insurance

Working with Your Board

We originally had a Board of five, but now, as a part of our succession planning, we have seven.

Your board members may bring good connections, investor confidence, and reputational strength, besides their individual unique skills and talents. They are there to see that the company is run responsibly. Hopefully, they will help with fundraising!

They also oversee legal compliance. They can offer independent input on strategy and resource allocation. They can act as a sounding board for perhaps difficult decisions. They can help develop succession plans.

Board of Directors meetings can be held in person or on Zoom. We have been having board meetings via Zoom since the Pandemic and have continued to do so to minimize travel time, even though all of our board members are in our county.

Insurance

A small, all-volunteer nonprofit primarily needs General Liability Insurance to cover accidents and property damage, plus Directors & Officers (D&O) Insurance to protect the leadership from lawsuits related to their management. Depending on operations, you may also need Professional Liability (E&O) for services, Commercial Property for owned or rented spaces, Commercial Auto for vehicles owned by your non-profit, and perhaps Cyber Liability for data security.

NIAC (Non-profit Insurance Alliance of California) should be your first stop (see Sources & Resources: NIAC) for insurance shopping in California. As their name would indicate, they issue insurance in California. See further info and link in the Sources & Resources section.

Office Space

We have found that we did not need a designated office for our non-profit charity. We have been able to run everything out of our home office. This surely is a cost savings.

The Best Solution to Hunger in America

In Summary

This area of legal affairs is complex and can be vexing. We can only say — stay with it. Once in place, you have the room to swing out and make a gigantic contribution to many, many people!

And we want to say from our hearts to you — call on us for help! With now twenty years under our belts, we are experts on this model of food rescue program and all its nuanced aspects.

Please look us up in the Sources & Resources section and be in touch.

We are here for YOU!

AT A GLANCE

- You need a nonprofit structure to partner with stores legally.
- Options: work under a church, a fiscal sponsor, or form your own 501(c)(3).
- Recruit a small, capable board — start with at least three officers.
- Consider insurance early (General Liability, D&O, Auto).
- Once your framework is in place, you can focus on community impact.

Chapter Eleven

Fundraising

One of the amazing features of this food distribution model is that the need for funds is small. Our entire program has been making it with minimal funding that comes primarily from individual donors in two main ways:

- "Financial Family" of sustainable monthly donations (see Monthly Donor Program below)
- 1-time end-of-year donations (see Annual Fundraising Campaign and Events below)

In addition, we have received some micro-grants (see below) over the years from:

- selected foundations
- local churches and stores where we pick up food
- banks

The organization does not get any government funding, so this program "does not cost the taxpayers a cent," as co-founder Curt Kinkead is fond of saying.

Each of these three distinct fundraising approaches funded approximately 1/3 of our annual budget. Taken together, our financial needs were covered.

See the How Much Money Do You Really Need section below.

Monthly Donor Program

We called this program our "Financial Family." The ground of being was that it was like a family, and we were taking care of our own in our county. We got it going by reaching out to our friends, folks we knew, and their friends. These monthly contributions are meant as sustainable long-term investments.

Some give as little as $10/month, and some give as much as $100/month. Totally, that yielded us $6,000 - $7,000/year.

On the tech side, we used online timesaving software—donorbox.org (see Sources & Resources: Donorbox). Donors can sign up for an electronic funds transfer directly from our website. It is automatic through Stripe, an online processing company, and also through PayPal. Most of the DonorBox features are free at their basic account level. However, some nifty add-ons will incur a fee (currently 2.95-3.95%). Link is in the Sources & Resources section at the end of this book.

There are other online donation software offerings, but Donorbox is our preference. We use the free version, and it seems to cover everything we need. They do have a premium plan, but it is more than what felt we needed or wanted to spend on such a tool.

Annual Fundraising Campaign & Events

We did a variety of different kinds of events over the years. We held acknowledgement and funding events in people's homes and in fun retail stores. We did an exclusive cocktail party for donors of $1000+ in an elegant home.

We held Christmas parties in December where we elicited donations from the volunteers because they, too, had benefited from the food they had received. We knew this created significant savings in their budgets.

Invitations to events were extended through emails. We made sure to make a pitch for those who couldn't make it to the events. But even in years without holiday events, we raised additional year-end funds through email and phone campaigns.

Each year, a team of 4-5 fundraisers would call their friends and also previous donors and request a year-end donation. We used donor lists so we would know what folks had contributed in the past. It enabled us to make larger requests.

We also made calls after the events to thank and acknowledge the contributions. Acknowledging our donors is one thing we were proud and happy to do! After all, they make the whole thing possible!

Pursuing Microgrants and Not Larger Grants

The reason we pursued smaller grants was that we have been an all-volunteer organization, so costs are low. AND, the larger grants require a lot of data collection and reporting, which we are not set up to do. It can be very time-consuming, and we decided not to take on that kind of task.

There are many $1,000 and $2,000+ grants that only require a simple application to be filled out with some documentation. We found they often say yes. And for some, the disbursements come annually just for updating the applications, especially with updated financial projections.

Also, keep your eyes out for awards. We applied several times and got rejected, but after several years, we did get a $5,000 award from our county's Center for Volunteer and Non-Profit Leadership. We pursued grants from the banks where we did our banking. We pursued stores where we pick up food. Whole Foods and Safeway have their own foundations, for example. Many companies, including real estate companies, have foundations, which we were able to access through our board members and volunteers.

We put together simple publicity materials to approach organizations for micro-grants. We set up folders where we included media articles about us, our 501(c)3 letter from the IRS, testimonials, and a simple three-page Frequently Asked Questions handout.

How Much Money Do You Really Need?

It is an ongoing, never-ending responsibility to make sure that the $1,500 to $2,000 per month that is needed actually shows up every month. As of 2025, the annual operation costs between $20,000 and $25,000.

The Best Solution to Hunger in America

This covers things like organizational and board insurance for liability, vehicle use reimbursement at $.70/mile, and minimal office expenses. We are looking at having the charity own its own vehicle. With that setup, Respecting Our Elders will be responsible for gas, tires, and servicing for that vehicle.

- Insurance: Currently about $2000 annually
- Annual Filing Fees: These are minimal ($25.00 every other year to the California Secretary of State's office
- Other Operational Expenses: Also minimal, approximately $300 a year
- Reimbursing Volunteers for Expenses and Mileage: Currently about $14,400. However, we are looking at the charity owning a van, and then this part of the budget will be applied to the purchase and then maintenance.

As you can imagine, it takes something to organize this three-pronged approach to fundraising. But what we want to say is that it definitely gets easier over the years.

AT A GLANCE

- Keep costs low so donations go directly to programs.
- Build a "Financial Family" — monthly donors who sustain you year-round.
- Supplement with micro-grants, local awards, and small foundation support.
- Hold community events to acknowledge donors and volunteers.
- Gratitude = retention — thank every donor personally.

Chapter Twelve

Marketing & Communications

Running a grassroots nonprofit isn't just about the hands-on work of serving people—it's also about keeping the lines of communication open. Whether you're connecting with donors, rallying volunteers, or building trust with the community, how you share your story can make or break your ability to grow and sustain your mission. In the beginning, communication may feel secondary to the "real work," but over time, you'll find it's what allows the real work to continue.

The following sections cover the essentials: building an online presence, maintaining relationships with the media, creating strong donor and volunteer communications, and using tools like email newsletters and social media to keep your organization alive in the hearts and minds of those who make it possible.

Website/Blog

We would say that having a website is really important. You will need an online presence, even if it is just a really basic site.

- It is a way to establish credibility and legitimacy.
- It is a way folks can find you and communicate with you via a Contact Us page.
- It is key to getting donations as well, with a Donate Here button or page. Many individual donors prefer to donate online rather than send checks.
- Finally, this is where your organization's branding will get established.

All of this is especially true if you are choosing to have your own non-profit charitable organization. If you are operating through a religious entity, hopefully, you will be able to post information on their site.

Media relations

With Respecting Our Elders, the media found us initially. It was a matter of local columnists looking for local stories of interest. Especially given the current situation in our country, with federal safety nets disappearing and affecting many programs designed to support financially challenged people, your story will likely be of interest.

We established relationships with some media people, and it is always good to mine any personal relationships that you and/or friends of the charity have.

With that said, our honest opinion is that articles and publicity haven't forwarded our cause very much. They might cause a flurry of interest and maybe a sprinkle of donations, but not worth a big investment of your time.

You will be able to use any articles or interviews in future PR, and so it will all contribute to sustaining your credibility.

Email newsletter

The first step is to create a mailing list that has segments for donors, volunteers, and friends of your organization.

It will be very important for you to be able to stay in touch with your audience.

Your audience will primarily be donors, friends of the organization, and volunteers.

To make your lists all work optimally and surely most easily, we'd recommend using one of the online email client systems, such as Mailchimp or MailerLite, or a similar one you may know about.

We do mostly email campaigns and found that quarterly communications that tell stories and share pictures (worth a thousand words) while acknowledging everyone involved was a high priority. You want to sustain your donors and volunteers and let folks know what's up that is making such a difference in the lives of people!

Handouts for Vendors

Vendors mean the stores or farmers, or food distributors who are giving you food.

We prepared professional materials for them in the form of a packet/folder of materials.

Items to include in such a packet:

- You need to prove that you are a legitimate 501(c)3 non-profit, so you need either your organization's own IRS letter or your religious non-profit's or fiscal sponsor's official paperwork.
- Be sure to include any articles written about your charitable successes.
- It is good to include any quotes from stores or food recipients, as you can gather those.
- And be sure to include your contact information, perhaps a business card.

Volunteer Communications

The main thing we want to emphasize here is to keep acknowledging your volunteers! It is vitally important for the good morale of your people that they feel truly valued for their participation.

In that regard, we do our best to get the volunteers together at least once a year, sometimes as fun holiday events of appreciation.

And then we also occasionally celebrated special occasions with the volunteers (and donors). For example, in December 2024, we gathered our volunteers for a holiday event, and in July 2025, we celebrated our 20th anniversary of the Respecting Our Elders charitable organization!

Donor Communications

We communicated with our donors primarily through a roughly quarterly newsletter.

As you probably know, there is a "season of giving" that is very real. It is basically from Thanksgiving through the holiday season, including New Year's Day.

It will behoove you to take good advantage of that and have a fundraising appeal happen during that window of time. People open their hearts and their pocketbooks, and your group may as well be one of the recipients of that generosity.

We reached out at other irregular times as well. For example, we fashioned a financial request with the initial gas hike because our expenses went up at that time. We also did a campaign around our 20th anniversary event to raise money to purchase a van.

In recent years, we have mostly communicated with donors by email. But occasionally, one of us will pick up the phone to either solicit or acknowledge a significant donation ($100 - $1,000+).

As charter investors in the Respecting Our Elders charity, we have closely witnessed the twenty-year successful unfolding of this food rescue program model. So many lives in Marin County have been impacted for the good! If you want to know how to create and run such a food program where you live, this book is for you!

– Fay Freed and Ronn Landsman

Social Media

Hopefully, someone on your team will be social media savvy. We say that because, as we're sure you know, it is a great tool for keeping a presence in the hearts and minds of folks. Communications can be posted on Facebook, Instagram, etc. And it is a lot to learn and know unless one has a social media knowledgeable guide.

AT A GLANCE

- Clear, steady communication keeps your mission alive.
- Maintain a simple website with a donation button and contact form.
- Use email newsletters to share stories and photos quarterly.
- Social media extends reach — delegate to a savvy volunteer if possible.
- Always acknowledge partners, volunteers, and donors publicly and sincerely.

Conclusion

When we began Respecting Our Elders, we didn't set out to create a model program. We simply wanted to make sure good food wasn't wasted and that our neighbors had what they needed. Over the years, something larger grew out of that simple idea.

Together with our volunteers and food donors, we built more than a food program. We built a community. Week after week, we have watched people move from worry and scarcity into a sense of sufficiency — and often into generosity. That transformation is just as important as the food itself.

Although we didn't intend to do so, we invented an assembly-line grade good karma generator that blesses everybody who comes near it. What started as a way to share food has become a source of health, purpose, and connection for everyone involved.

The results have surprised even us. We've seen seniors stay healthier, families make ends meet, and friendships form that would not have existed otherwise. In a county with one of the largest senior populations in California, our volunteers and recipients have shown that neighbors helping neighbors can be a powerful force for good.

Looking back after twenty years, we are grateful. Grateful to the stores that trust us with their donations, to the volunteers who give their time and energy, and to the recipients who remind us every day that dignity and respect matter. Most of all, I am grateful that something so simple — rescuing food that would otherwise be thrown away — can change so many lives for the better.

The Best Solution to Hunger in America

Most of all, we are grateful that something so simple—rescuing food that would otherwise be thrown away—can change so many lives for the better.

If this book helps you start a program of your own, we believe you'll find the same truth we did: When a community comes together to share what it has, everyone thrives.

Sources & Further Resources

Throughout this handbook, we've referenced key data and reports to help ground our model in the larger context of food insecurity, food waste, and community-based solutions. Below is a list of these sources, organized by topic, with links for further exploration.

Food Waste in America

U.S. Environmental Protection Agency (EPA) – United States 2030 Food Loss and Waste Reduction Goal
epa.gov/sustainable-management-food/united-states-2030-food-loss-and-waste-reduction-goal

Link to EPA food waste triangle graphic:
epa.gov/smm/sustainable-materials-management-non-hazardous-materials-and-waste-management-hierarchy

U.S. Department of Agriculture (USDA) – Food Loss and Waste Overview usda.gov/foodlossandwaste

Recycling and Trash Solutions (RTS) – Food Waste in America: 2024 Guide rts.com/resources/guides/food-waste-america/

Food Waste in America – Statistics and Impacts (EPA and USDA Joint Statement and Supporting Reports)
epa.gov/sustainable-management-food

Federal Resources

How to apply for 501c3 status with the IRS
https://www.irs.gov/charities-non-profits/how-to-apply-for-501c3status#:~:text=To%20apply%20for%20recognition%20by,Updated:%2020%2DAug%2D2025

IRS Publication 4303: A Donor's Guide to Vehicle Donation
irs.gov/pub/irs-pdf/p4303.pdf

Bill Emerson Good Samaritan Food Donation Act
usda.gov/sites/default/files/documents/us-food-donation-act-of-2021.pdf

California Reports, Law & Regulations

California SB1383: Short-Lived Climate Pollutant Reduction Law
calrecycle.ca.gov/organics/slcp

Map the Meal Gap 2025: Feeding America Report
feedingamerica.org/sites/default/files/2025-05/Map%20the%20Meal%20Gap%202025%20Report.pdf

CALMatters Report on Federal Food Program Cuts (2025)
marinij.com/2025/04/09/federal-cuts-threaten-food-bank-programs/

Marin County Specific Resources

Marin County Food System Assessment Project (2012), prepared by David Haskell and funded by the Marin Community Foundation. marinfoodsystem.wordpress.com/wp-content/uploads/2012/02/marin-county-food-system-assessement-project-report.pdf

Study: Thousands of Marin seniors among state's hidden poor (updated July 19, 2018)
marinij.com/2015/09/07/study-thousands-of-marin-seniors-among-states-hidden-poor/

Organizational & Operational Tools

Nolo Press: How to Form a Nonprofit Corporation (National Edition): A Step-by-Step Guide to Forming a 501(c)(3) Nonprofit in Any State nolo.com

Nonprofit Insurance Alliance of California (NIAC)
insurancefornonprofits.org

Donorbox Online Fundraising Platform donorbox.org

Respecting Our Elders documents, including our Volunteer handbook and agreements, Articles of Incorporation, and bylaws Please send an email to ruth@respectingourelders.org to request these files.

Additional Recommended Reading

Bloom, Jonathan. *American Wasteland: How America Throws Away Nearly Half of Its Food (and What We Can Do About It)* (Da Capo Press, 2010) americanwastelandbook.com/

Stuart, Tristram. *Waste: Uncovering the Global Food Scandal* (W. W. Norton & Company, 2009) tristramstuart.co.uk/books

Martin, Katie S. *Reinventing Food Banks and Pantries: New Tools to End Hunger* (Island Press, 2021) islandpress.org/books/reinventing-food-banks-and-pantries

All of these books are available through major online retailers, or your favorite local bookstore.

To access a digital version of this Sources & Further Resources section, just go to:

respectingourelders.org/resources.

Community Advisors and Support Network

One of the goals of this handbook is to help create a nationwide network of local food rescue programs modeled after Respecting Our Elders. To support that mission, we are making ourselves and our trusted advisors available to assist others getting started.

Ruth Schwartz and Curt Kinkead, founders of Respecting Our Elders, can provide guidance on forming and running an all-volunteer food rescue organization—from recruiting and managing volunteers and store partnerships to sustainability and community engagement. Email: ruth@respectingourelders.org

Fay Freed, a longtime volunteer and experienced fundraising consultant, is available to advise on establishing donor programs and fundraising campaigns that support your nonprofit's growth. She has been our advisor from the very beginning, helping us meet our financial goals every year. Email: faysfreed@gmail.com

In keeping with our all-volunteer model, we offer our time and expertise freely to help others start or strengthen their own community food rescue programs. If our support proves valuable, we simply ask that you consider a donation to Respecting Our Elders as a gesture of reciprocity — helping us continue to nourish people and share this model with others.

www.ingramcontent.com/pod-product-compliance
Lightning Source LLC
Chambersburg PA
CBHW060033040426
42333CB00042B/2408